The
Coloring
Devotional

Thunder Bay Press
An imprint of Printers Row Publishing Group
9717 Pacific Heights Blvd, San Diego, CA 92121
www.thunderbaybooks.com • mail@thunderbaybooks.com

Thunder Bay Press
Publisher: Peter Norton
Associate Publisher: Ana Parker
Editor: Dan Mansfield

Produced by:
The Bright Press, an imprint of The Quarto Group
Publisher: James Evans
Editorial Director: Isheeta Mustafi
Managing Editor: Jacqui Sayers
Editors: Abbie Sharman and Kathleen Steeden
Designer: Wheel Design

Author: Rachel Mayew
Illustrator: Sarah Skeate

ISBN: 978-1-6672-0050-7

Printed in China

27 26 25 24 23   1 2 3 4 5

The Coloring Devotional

Inspiring Bible Verses to Color

Rachel Mayew

THUNDER BAY
P · R · E · S · S

San Diego, California

Contents

This book is divided into seven chapters, each of which focuses on a different theme, from finding inner peace to living mindfully. The coloring pages are accompanied by corresponding journaling sections at the end of each chapter. There are 52 reflections pages—one for each week of the year—so you can build your regular devotional coloring practice.

Introduction

I'm so glad you're here.

Even now, as you read this introduction, you are likely pausing to consider how you might welcome more peace into your life. Or perhaps you're wondering whether you might gift this book to another, to encourage them to be intentional about their own inner peace. These precious pauses are the very basis of this book and the offering it brings.

It's not often we look at the day ahead and truly expect to find deep inner peace. We aren't gifted an abundance of days without obstacles or demands, but, as Christians, we are offered a higher path. We're called to take thoughts captive, to be transformed by the renewing of our minds, and to think on higher things. By intentionally putting these acts into practice, the God of peace goes with us, improving our mental, emotional, and spiritual health (see 2 Corinthians 10:5, Romans 12:2, Philippians 4:4–9).

Over the years, I've found that to keep my heart open to God's gifts, I need to institute routines of remembrance that support my heart and mind. None of it is too intricate or time-consuming. In fact, with God meeting me in these practices, I find I merely need the discipline to keep showing up. Aiding in this intentional faithfulness is where I believe this book becomes of service. There is an intentional, actional portion of our faith relationship that is solely our responsibility. It is that of choosing a response to

God's grace, to lean in and look within, to seek God above all the noise. Then, quite incredibly, it is God who does the heavy lifting. It is here in this divine give and take that lasting change begins and is upheld.

The Coloring Devotional gives you an easy, practical way to make the choice of connecting with God a consistent part of your daily routine. Having a way to put this choice into action is a big part of the equation. Just reaching for this book and taking out fresh colors will hopefully spark a little joy all on its own. Combining the creative and soothing aspects of coloring with ancient scriptural text enables a gentle transition from the busyness of the mind into quiet communion with God, where true peace abounds.

Each day we tend to get caught in the push and pull between grace and chaos, activity and rest. Incorporating mindfulness allows us to lift our attention away from daily demands, ease anxiety and worry, and create more space for God's good gifts.

I am expectantly joyful for you as you commit to showing up and choosing peace!

Be blessed.

Rachel

How to use this book

Each section of this book is designed to lead you to inner peace. The Bible passages and scriptural affirmations found on each beautiful coloring page have been curated and grouped together thematically, so that as you move through this book, you can easily find a topic and verse that meets you right where you are that day. At the end of each chapter, you'll find reflection pages for the verses, providing space for you to record your takeaways and observations.

The art mediums you use for coloring are, of course, your choice and can vary from session to session. Many people enjoy using colored pencils, as these allow you to layer and build color, starting lightly and, as you move outward, applying more pressure to deepen the hue.

My biggest tip, though, is to set the scene for yourself when you sit down to use this book. We're so used to being busy and striving to move forward. Countless external distractions and our own frantic thoughts seem to go on without end. As this pace becomes our norm, it can require a lot of effort to slow down, breathe, and notice. It takes time to retrain the brain so that it feels safe and rewarded by this strange new stillness. But being intentional about using all five senses as you use this book will tell the mind, "Yes, we're slowing down. Yes, it is intentional!"

Select a suitable time of day and a comfortable setting and remove as many distractions as possible. Taste and smell are also powerful, so you may like to bring a cup of tea or another beverage to this space. Be sure to inhale the aromas before taking a sip. Lighting a candle is also a great way to add ambience and bring intentionality to your mindful Scripture-coloring practice.

Begin with a short prayer to welcome God into this moment and read through the verse or affirmation on your selected page. Don't trouble yourself too much with selecting your colors. Let your inner child play and have fun with this activity! The sights of the colors as they fill the page will give your mind a steady place to rest. You may like to repeat the verse out loud or silently, or simply set the intention of making space for the promise of the quotation to take root in your spirit. As thoughts, images, and distractions come up, choose to view them with gratitude and release them to God, trusting peace will come in that area.

It is my prayer that as you use this book to meet with God, you also meet a deeper part of yourself. I also hope that in reading and coloring with these verses, which are words that God has imparted to you, you improve the health of your mind, body, and spirit, finding peace in every part of your life.

CHAPTER 1

Find Inner Peace

It is such a gift to be given inner peace, to know this is not something you must work to manifest, but rather part of your inheritance as a child of God. Jesus says to those who follow after God that he grants them his own peace. The peace of proximity to God supported Jesus as he navigated daily life on earth, facing a range of difficulties, from ministering to mass crowds to loneliness and, ultimately, the cross. And that same peace is granted to you! Take heart in knowing no matter how difficult the season, you are sustained through it all by the peace that surpasses all understanding.

God's peace guards my heart and mind

Let
the peace
of God
rule in your
heart

Peace I leave with you. My peace I give to you.

God's peace
blesses
me in all
things

Peace
and loving
kindness

are constants in my life

My soul rests in God

We have **peace** with **God**

Peace, be still

I am
blessed
with every
spiritual
blessing

Nothing separates me from God's love

Page 11
PHILIPPIANS 4:6–7 *(WEB)*

In nothing be anxious, but in everything, by prayer and petition with thanksgiving, let your requests be made known to God.
And the peace of God, which surpasses all understanding, will guard your hearts and your thoughts in Christ Jesus.

In what situation do you need to follow these instructions and trust God for peace?

_____

_____

_____

_____

_____

_____

This week I am thankful for

_____

_____

_____

_____

_____

_____

_____

_____

Special thoughts

_____

_____

_____

_____

_____

_____

_____

_____

Page 13
COLOSSIANS 3:14–15 *(WEB)*

Above all these things, walk in love, which is the bond of perfection. And let the peace of God rule in your hearts, to which also you were called in one body, and be thankful.

_____

_____

_____

_____

_____

_____

_____

Page 14
JOHN 14:27 *(DRB)*

Peace I leave with you, my peace I give unto you: not as the world giveth, do I give unto you. Let not your heart be troubled, nor let it be afraid.

_____

_____

_____

_____

_____

_____

_____

Page 17
1 THESSALONIANS 5:23 *(DRB)*

And may the God of peace himself sanctify you in all things: that your whole spirit and soul and body may be preserved blameless in the coming of our Lord Jesus Christ.

_____

_____

_____

_____

_____

_____

_____

_____

Page 19
ISAIAH 54:10 *(WEB)*

For the mountains may depart,
   and the hills be removed;
but my loving kindness will not depart from you,
   and my covenant of peace will not be removed.

_____

_____

_____

_____

_____

_____

_____

PSALM 62:1–6 (WEB)

My soul rests in God alone.
    My salvation is from him.
He alone is my rock, my salvation, and my fortress.
    I will never be greatly shaken.
How long will you assault a man?
    Would all of you throw him down,
    like a leaning wall, like a tottering fence?
They fully intend to throw him down from his lofty place.
    They delight in lies.
    They bless with their mouth, but they curse inwardly. *Selah.*
My soul, wait in silence for God alone,
    for my expectation is from him.
He alone is my rock and my salvation, my fortress.
    I will not be shaken.

Note and pray on where you should put expectations on God alone.

_____

_____

_____

This week I am thankful for   *Special thoughts*

_____   _____

_____   _____

_____   _____

_____   _____

_____   _____

_____   _____

Page 23
ROMANS 5:1 *(KJV)*

Therefore being justified by faith, we have peace with God through our Lord Jesus Christ.

_____

_____

_____

_____

_____

_____

_____

Page 24
MARK 4:39 *(KJV)*

And he arose, and rebuked the wind, and said unto the sea, Peace, be still. And the wind ceased, and there was a great calm.

_____

_____

_____

_____

_____

_____

_____

_____

Page 27
EPHESIANS 1:3 *(WEB)*

Blessed be the God and Father of our Lord Jesus Christ, who has blessed us with every spiritual blessing in the heavenly places in Christ.

_____

_____

_____

_____

_____

_____

_____

Page 29
ROMANS 8:38–39 *(KJV)*

For I am persuaded, that neither death, nor life, nor angels, nor principalities, nor powers, nor things present, nor things to come,
Nor height, nor depth, nor any other creature, shall be able to separate us from the love of God, which is in Christ Jesus our Lord.

_____

_____

_____

_____

_____

_____

_____

CHAPTER 2

Do Not Be Afraid

Have you heard it said that there are enough verses telling us to not be afraid that a different one could be read each day of the year without any repeats? Regardless of the exact count, this message is reiterated for a reason. God knew none of us would walk through life without facing fearful things, but still desired and planned a higher way for each of us. So what's the secret? How are you to fear not when life gets scary? First, rest in knowing God does not hold an impossible expectation of you, but instead gifts you with divine courage and strength. When troubles arise, anchor yourself in the truths that follow and be equipped to move forward with wisdom, peace, and confidence.

Cast all your worries on God because **he cares for you**

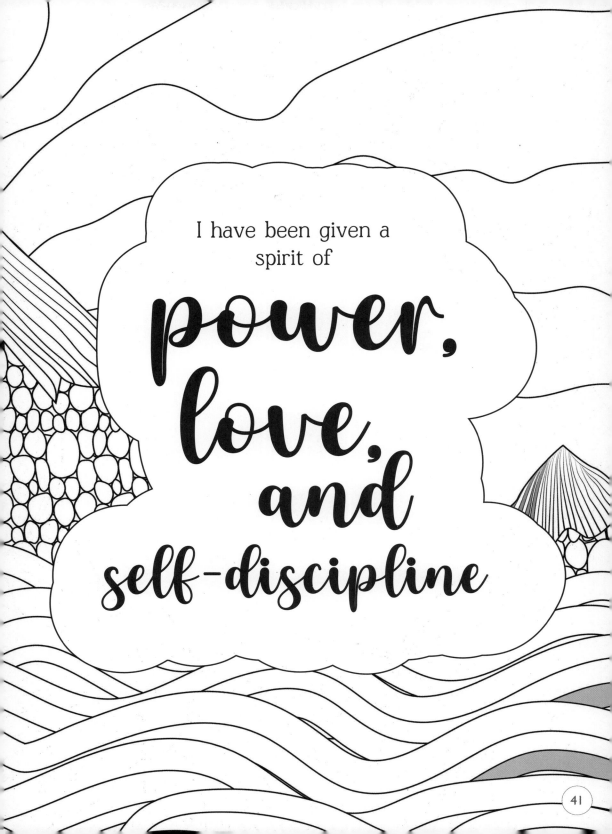

I have been given a spirit of

power,
love,
and
self-discipline

The Lord bless you, and keep you

I do not fear. I am not afraid.

Be strong and of good courage

God is with me, and I fear nothing

I dwell in safety with my God

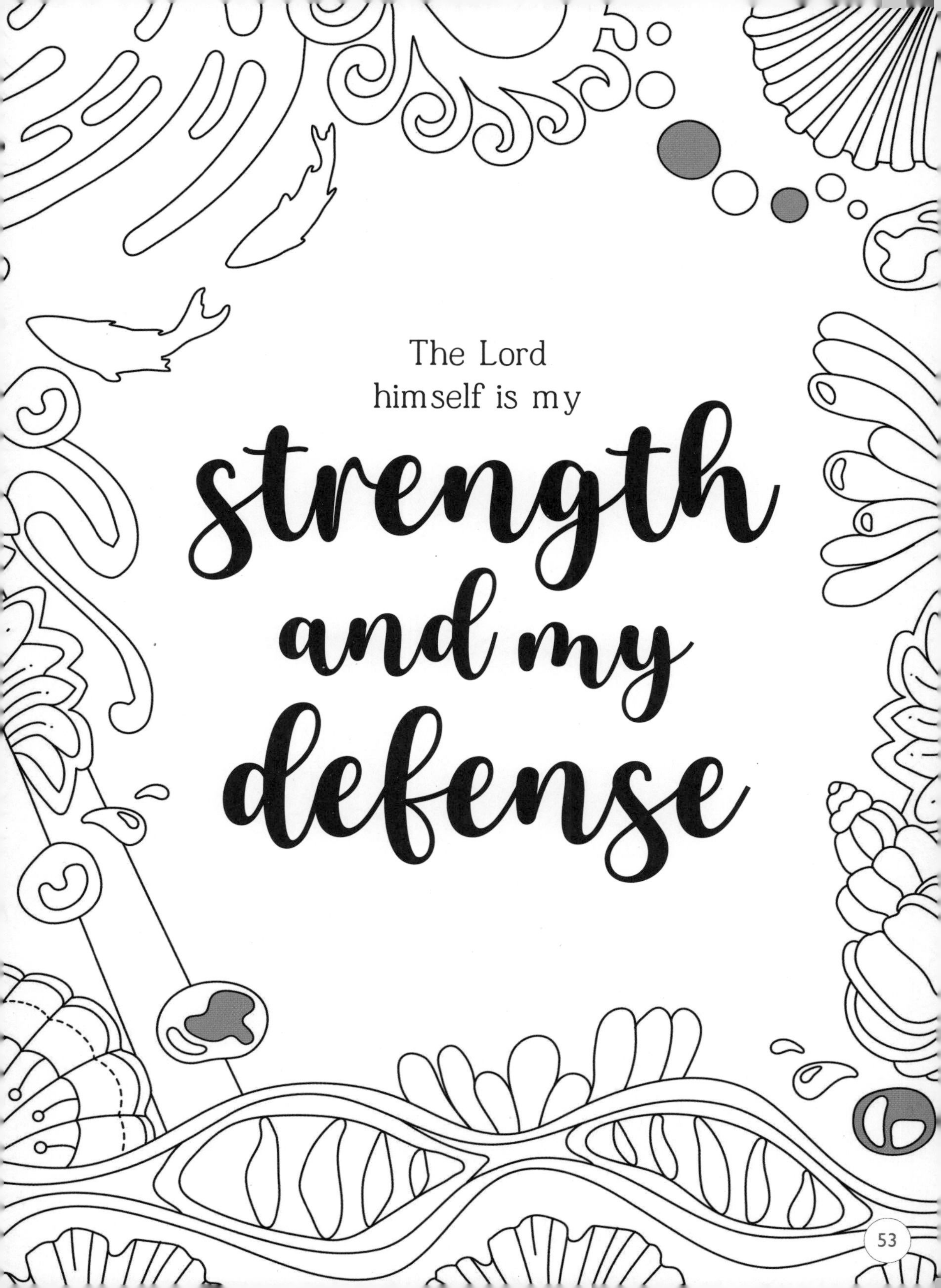

The Lord
himself is my

strength
and my
defense

In God
I trust,
and I am
not afraid

Do not be dismayed, for

I am your God

God holds me by the right hand

Page 39
I PETER 5:6–7 *(WEB)*

Humble yourselves therefore under the mighty hand of God, that he may exalt you in due time, casting all your worries on him, because he cares for you.

_____

_____

_____

_____

_____

_____

_____

Page 41
2 TIMOTHY 1:7 *(WEB)*

For God didn't give us a spirit of fear, but of power, love, and self-control.

_____

_____

_____

_____

_____

_____

_____

Page 42
NUMBERS 6:24–26 *(WEB)*

God bless you, and keep you.
God make his face to shine on you,
    and be gracious to you.
God lift up his face toward you,
    and give you peace.

How do these verses diminish your fears?

_____

_____

_____

_____

_____

This week I am thankful for

_____

_____

_____

_____

_____

_____

_____

Special thoughts

_____

_____

_____

_____

_____

_____

_____

Page 45
DEUTERONOMY 31:6 *(KJV)*

Be strong and of a good courage, fear not, nor be afraid of them: for the Lord thy God, he it is that doth go with thee; he will not fail thee, nor forsake thee.

_____

_____

_____

_____

_____

_____

Page 47
JOSHUA 1:9 *(KJV)*

Have not I commanded thee? Be strong and of a good courage; be not afraid, neither be thou dismayed: for the Lord thy God is with thee whithersoever thou goest.

_____

_____

_____

_____

_____

_____

Page 48
PSALM 23:4–5 *(WEB)*

Even though I walk through the valley of the shadow of death,
 I will fear no evil, for you are with me.
Your rod and your staff,
 they comfort me.
You prepare a table before me
 in the presence of my enemies.
You anoint my head with oil.
 My cup runs over.

In what situation can you trust God deeply for rest, provision, and peace?

_____

_____

_____

_____

_____

_____

This week I am thankful for

_____

_____

_____

_____

_____

Special thoughts

_____

_____

_____

_____

_____

Page 51
PSALM 4:8 *(WEB)*

In peace I will both lay myself down and sleep,
   for you, God alone, make me live in safety.

_____

_____

_____

_____

_____

_____

_____

Page 53
ISAIAH 12:2 *(WEB)*

Behold, God is my salvation. I will trust, and will not be afraid; for God is my
strength and song; and he has become my salvation.

_____

_____

_____

_____

_____

_____

_____

Page 55
PSALM 56:3-4 (WEB)

When I am afraid,
    I will put my trust in you.
In God, I praise his word.
    In God, I put my trust.
I will not be afraid.
    What can flesh do to me?

Write out praise to God that you can repeat to give you courage when you're afraid.

_____

_____

_____

_____

This week I am thankful for   Special thoughts

_____   _____

_____   _____

_____   _____

_____   _____

_____   _____

_____   _____

_____   _____

_____   _____

Pages 56 and 58
ISAIAH 41:10 & 13 (WEB)

Don't you be afraid, for I am with you.
　Don't be dismayed, for I am your God.
　I will strengthen you.
　Yes, I will help you.
　Yes, I will uphold you with the right hand of my righteousness.
…
For I, your God, will hold your right hand,
　saying to you, "Don't be afraid.
　I will help you."

Journal or draw what trusting that God is with you looks like in your current situation.

_____

_____

_____

_____

_____

_____

_____

_____

_____

_____

_____

_____

This week I am thankful for

_____

_____

_____

_____

_____

_____

_____

_____

_____

_____

_____

_____

_____

_____

_____

_____

Special thoughts

_____

_____

_____

_____

_____

_____

_____

_____

_____

_____

_____

_____

_____

_____

_____

CHAPTER 3

Achieve Balance

Longing to achieve balance may seem like a modern complexity, but there are many passages from which you can glean biblical wisdom on the topic. From reminders on how your identity does not lie in external factors to guidance on managing a healthy thought life, it is clear that your overall well-being matters to God. And when something matters to God, gifts are bestowed. So rest assured, being anchored in the verses that follow will equip you to navigate the path ahead, walk in wisdom, redeem your time, and finally achieve the balance you've been craving.

Let your
speech be gracious;

season

your words

with

salt

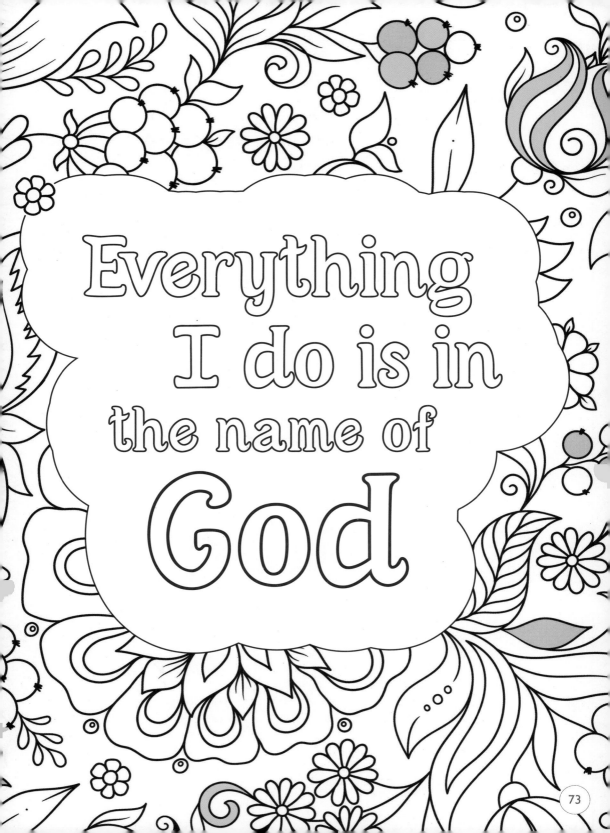

Everything
I do is in
the name of
God

Act justly, love mercy, and **walk humbly with your God**

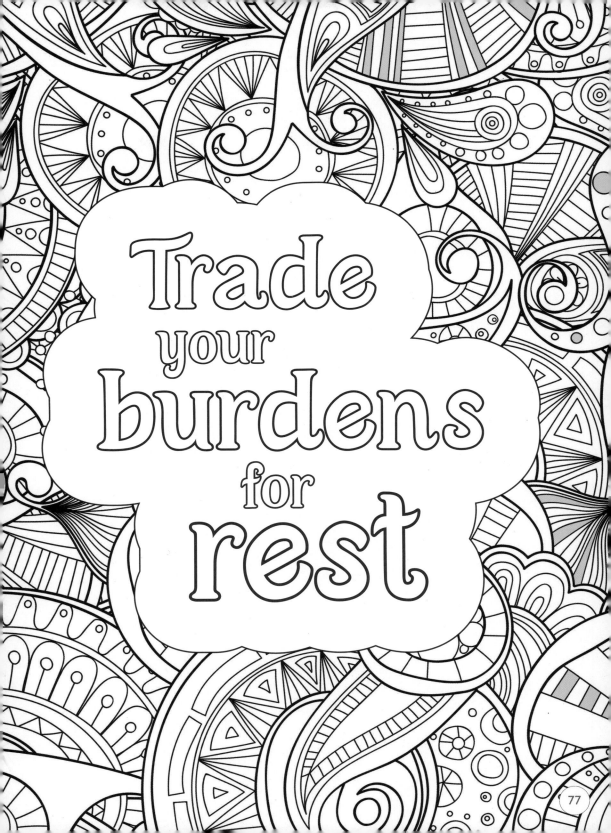

Trade your burdens for rest

I return to God and am saved by his rest

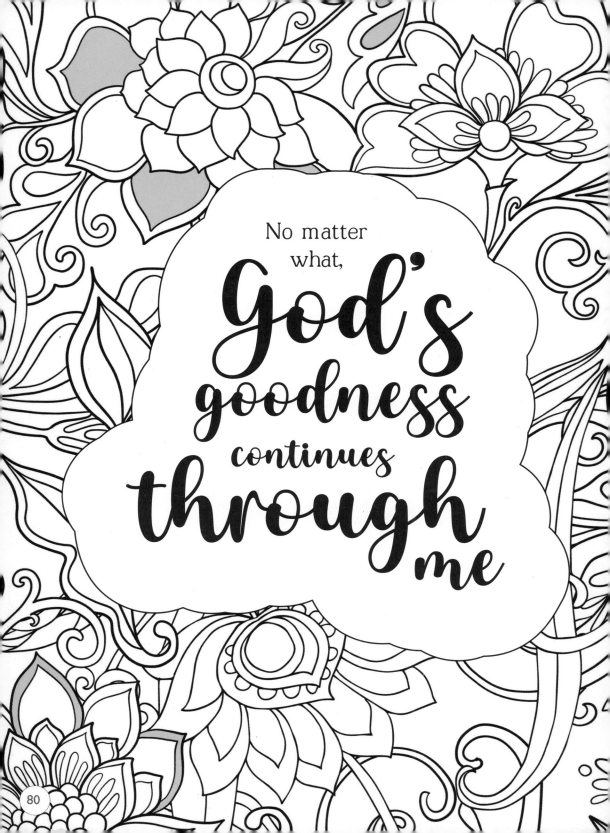

No matter what, God's goodness continues through me

When I am **weak,**
I am **strong**

Find beauty in all things

Trust in God's timing

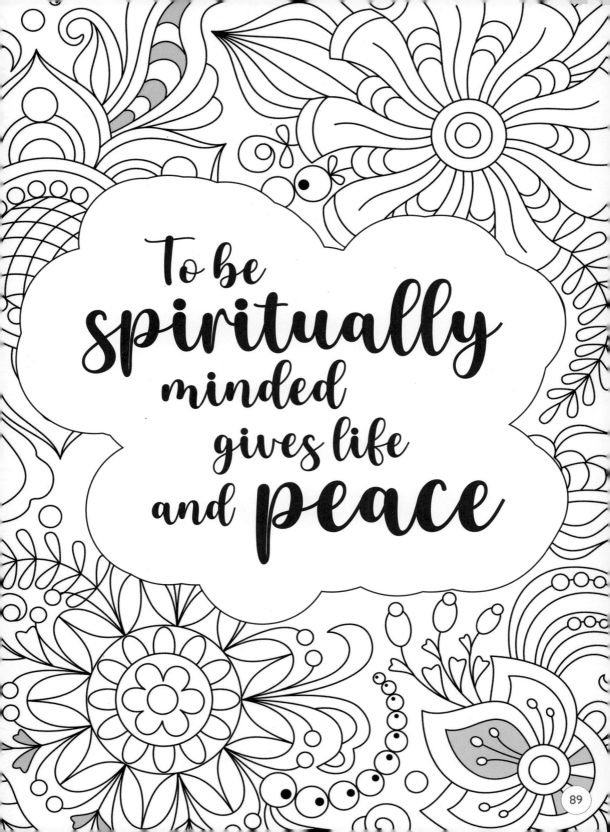

To be **spiritually** minded gives life and **peace**

Page 70
COLOSSIANS 4:6 *(WEB)*

Let your speech always be with grace, seasoned with salt, that you may know how you ought to answer each one.

_____

_____

_____

_____

_____

_____

_____

Page 73
COLOSSIANS 3:17 *(WEB)*

Whatever you do, in word or in deed, do all in the name of the Lord Jesus, giving thanks to God the Father, through him.

_____

_____

_____

_____

_____

_____

_____

Page 74
MICAH 6:8 (WEB)

He has shown you, O man, what is good.
  What does God require of you, but to act justly,
  to love mercy, and to walk humbly with your God?

Do these requirements feel easy or hard? Write God a prayer of response.

_____

_____

_____

_____

This week I am thankful for   *Special thoughts*

_____   _____

_____   _____

_____   _____

_____   _____

_____   _____

_____   _____

_____   _____

_____   _____

Page 77
MATTHEW 11:28 *(WEB)*

Come to me, all you who labor and are heavily burdened, and I will give you rest.

_____

_____

_____

_____

_____

_____

_____

Page 79
ISAIAH 30:15 *(WEB)*

For thus said the Lord God, the Holy One of Israel, "You will be saved in returning and rest."

_____

_____

_____

_____

_____

_____

_____

PHILIPPIANS 1:3–6 *(WEB)*

I thank my God whenever I remember you, always in every request of mine on behalf of you all, making my requests with joy, for your partnership in furtherance of the Good News from the first day until now; being confident of this very thing, that he who began a good work in you will complete it until the day of Jesus Christ.

Where in your life can you cease striving and trust God's work?

_____

_____

_____

_____

_____

This week I am thankful for

_____

_____

_____

_____

_____

_____

_____

Special thoughts

_____

_____

_____

_____

_____

_____

_____

Page 83
2 CORINTHIANS 12:10 *(WEB)*

Therefore I take pleasure in weaknesses, in injuries, in necessities, in persecutions, and in distresses, for Christ's sake. For when I am weak, then am I strong.

_____

_____

_____

_____

_____

_____

_____

_____

Page 85
ECCLESIASTES 3:11 *(WEB)*

He has made everything beautiful in its time. He has also set eternity in their hearts, yet so that man can't find out the work that God has done from the beginning even to the end.

_____

_____

_____

_____

_____

_____

Page 86
ECCLESIASTES 3:1 *(YLT)*

To everything—a season, and a time to every delight under the heavens.

_____

_____

_____

_____

_____

_____

_____

Page 89
ROMANS 8:4–6 *(DRA)*

That the justification of the law might be fulfilled in us, who walk not according to the flesh, but according to the spirit.
For they that are according to the flesh, mind the things that are of the flesh; but they that are according to the spirit, mind the things that are of the spirit.
For the wisdom of the flesh is death; but the wisdom of the spirit is life and peace.

_____

_____

_____

_____

_____

_____

_____

CHAPTER 4

Bless Others

It is widely known that helping others brings a sense of peace and well-being. Immerse yourself in these verses not only to be encouraged to bless others but to be reminded of just how blessed you are. Getting a glimpse of all that's been given by God and all that continues to flow into your life is an incredibly empowering way to fulfill your desire to care for God's creation and truly bless others.

With
God,
I lack no
good
thing

Blessed are the peacemakers

Charity bonds us in perfect love

Do what is good for one another

Pursue peace in all things with all people

The
fruit
of justice
is sown in
peace

Create peace and build one another up

Be kind to one another, forgiving each other

Freely you received, so freely give

Love one another as God has loved you

Showing
love,
bear
one another's
burdens

MATTHEW 6:33 (WEB)

But seek first God's Kingdom and his righteousness; and all these things will be given to you as well.

How does believing this equip you to be generous with others?

_____

_____

_____

_____

_____

_____

_____

This week I am thankful for

_____

_____

_____

_____

_____

_____

_____

Special thoughts

_____

_____

_____

_____

_____

_____

_____

Page 101
MATTHEW 5:5–9 (WEB)

Blessed are the gentle,
    for they shall inherit the earth.
Blessed are those who hunger and thirst for righteousness,
    for they shall be filled.
Blessed are the merciful,
    for they shall obtain mercy.
Blessed are the pure in heart,
    for they shall see God.
Blessed are the peacemakers,
    for they shall be called children of God.

How does living and being blessed this way improve your relationships?

_____

_____

_____

This week I am thankful for

_____

_____

_____

_____

_____

_____

Special thoughts

_____

_____

_____

_____

_____

_____

Page 102
COLOSSIANS 3:13–16 *(KJV)*

Forbearing one another, and forgiving one another, if any man have a quarrel against any: even as Christ forgave you, so also do ye.
And above all these things put on charity, which is the bond of perfectness.
And let the peace of God rule in your hearts, to the which also ye are called in one body; and be ye thankful.
Let the word of Christ dwell in you richly in all wisdom; teaching and admonishing one another in psalms and hymns and spiritual songs, singing with grace in your hearts to the Lord.

Read this passage a few times and note what resonates with you most.

_____

_____

_____

This week I am thankful for   *Special thoughts*

Page 105
I THESSALONIANS 5:15 *(WEB)*

See that no one returns evil for evil to anyone, but always follow after that which is good for one another and for all.

_____

_____

_____

_____

_____

_____

_____

_____

Page 107
HEBREWS 12:14 *(DBY)*

Pursue peace with all, and holiness, without which no one shall see the Lord.

_____

_____

_____

_____

_____

_____

_____

_____

Page 108
JAMES 3:17–18 (DRA)

But the wisdom, that is from above, first indeed is chaste, then peaceable, modest, easy to be persuaded, consenting to the good, full of mercy and good fruits, without judging, without dissimulation.
And the fruit of justice is sown in peace, to them that make peace.

_____

_____

_____

_____

_____

_____

Page 111
PROVERBS 12:18–20 (WEB)

There is one who speaks rashly like the piercing of a sword,
    but the tongue of the wise heals.
Truth's lips will be established forever,
    but a lying tongue is only momentary.
Deceit is in the heart of those who plot evil,
    but joy comes to the promoters of peace.

_____

_____

_____

_____

_____

Page 112
ROMANS 14:19 *(DBY)*

So then let us pursue the things which tend to peace, and things whereby one shall build up another.

_____

_____

_____

_____

_____

_____

Page 115
EPHESIANS 4:32 *(WEB)*

And be kind to one another, tender hearted, forgiving each other, just as God also in Christ forgave you.

_____

_____

_____

_____

_____

_____

_____

Page 117
MATTHEW 10:7–8 (WEB)

As you go, preach, saying, "The Kingdom of Heaven is at hand!" Heal the sick, cleanse the lepers, and cast out demons. Freely you received, so freely give.

What have you freely received from God that you can now share?

_____

_____

_____

_____

_____

This week I am thankful for

_____

_____

_____

_____

_____

_____

_____

_____

Special thoughts

_____

_____

_____

_____

_____

_____

_____

_____

Page 119
JOHN 15:12–15 *(WEB)*

This is my commandment, that you love one another, even as I have loved you. Greater love has no one than this, that someone lay down his life for his friends. You are my friends, if you do whatever I command you. No longer do I call you servants, for the servant doesn't know what his lord does. But I have called you friends, for everything that I heard from my Father, I have made known to you.

_____

_____

_____

_____

_____

_____

_____

_____

Page 120
GALATIANS 6:2 *(DBY)*

Bear one another's burdens, and thus fulfill the law of the Christ.

_____

_____

_____

_____

_____

_____

_____

CHAPTER 5

Be Strong

With so much push and pull in the world, and so many messages
clamoring for your attention, it is easy to feel tossed about.
But in God you are more than a conqueror; you will not be moved and
can do all things through Christ, who strengthens you. Use this chapter
when you need to be reminded of where your strength comes from
and find the courage to do what God is calling you to do in this season.

Let us always consider love and good works

134

Stand firm in your faith! Be courageous! Be strong!

May the
Lord
give you
peace
at all
times

137

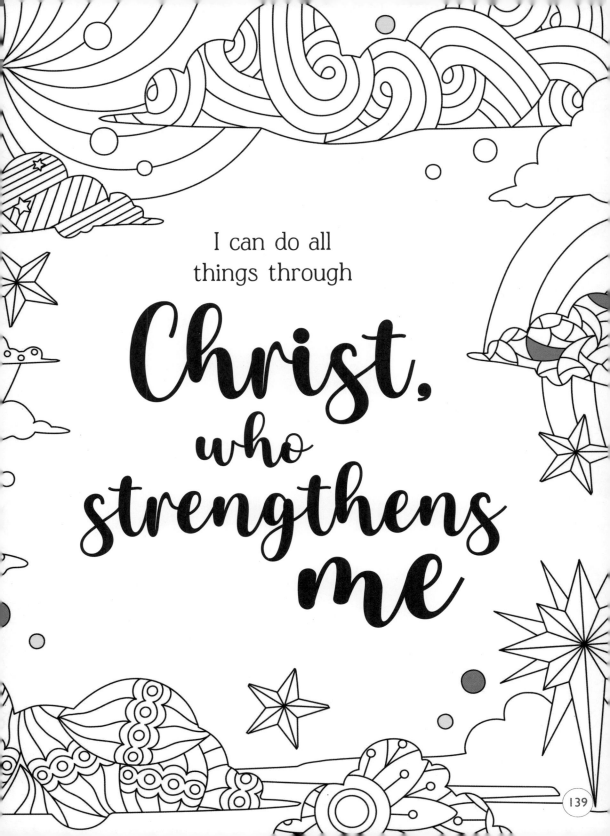

I can do all
things through
Christ,
who
strengthens
me

Trials only build my endurance

My mind is steadfast

and kept in

perfect

peace

143

I am **more** than a conqueror

I hope in
the
Lord
and he renews my
strength

I will not be moved

God
is not a
God
of
disorder but of
peace

Page 133
HEBREWS 10:24 *(WEB)*

Let's consider how to provoke one another to love and good works.

How can making this your focus also make you strong?

_____

_____

_____

_____

_____

_____

_____

This week I am thankful for

_____

_____

_____

_____

_____

_____

_____

_____

Special thoughts

_____

_____

_____

_____

_____

_____

_____

_____

1 CORINTHIANS 16:13–14 (WEB)

Watch! Stand firm in the faith! Be courageous! Be strong! Let all that you do be done in love.

_____

_____

_____

_____

_____

_____

_____

2 THESSALONIANS 3:16 (WEB)

Now may the Lord of peace himself give you peace at all times in all ways. The Lord be with you all.

_____

_____

_____

_____

_____

_____

PHILIPPIANS 4:12–13 *(WEB)*

I know how to be humbled, and I also know how to abound. In everything and in all things I have learned the secret both to be filled and to be hungry, both to abound and to be in need. I can do all things through Christ, who strengthens me.

Where might you be strengthened if you relied more heavily on God?

_____

_____

_____

_____

_____

This week I am thankful for

Special thoughts

Page 140
JAMES 1:3–4 (WEB)

Knowing that the testing of your faith produces endurance. Let endurance have its perfect work, that you may be perfect and complete, lacking in nothing.

In which areas of your life do you feel tested right now? How are you growing through these experiences?

_____

_____

_____

_____

_____

This week I am thankful for

_____

_____

_____

_____

_____

_____

_____

Special thoughts

_____

_____

_____

_____

_____

_____

_____

Page 143
ISAIAH 26:3–4 *(WEB)*

You will keep whoever's mind is steadfast in perfect peace,
    because he trusts in you.
Trust in God forever;
    for in God is an everlasting Rock.

In what situation do you crave stability? Write a short prayer of trust to God.

_____

_____

_____

_____

_____

This week I am thankful for   *Special thoughts*

Page 144
ROMANS 8:37 *(WEB)*

No, in all these things, we are more than conquerors through him who loved us.

_____

_____

_____

_____

_____

_____

_____

_____

_____

Page 147
ISAIAH 40:31 *(DRA)*

But they that hope in the Lord shall renew their strength, they shall take wings as eagles, they shall run and not be weary, they shall walk and not faint.

_____

_____

_____

_____

_____

_____

_____

Page 148
PSALM 125:1–2 (WEB)

Those who trust in God are as Mount Zion,
  which can't be moved, but remains forever.
As the mountains surround Jerusalem,
  so God surrounds his people from this time forward and forever more.

Where could you stand to trust God more, knowing you'll receive strength?

_____

_____

_____

_____

_____

This week I am thankful for   *Special thoughts*

_____   _____

_____   _____

_____   _____

_____   _____

_____   _____

_____   _____

_____   _____

1 CORINTHIANS 14:32–33 (WEB)

The spirits of the prophets are subject to the prophets, for God is not a God of confusion, but of peace, as in all the assemblies of the saints.

Write a short prayer you can come back to when you face confusion and disorder.

_____

_____

_____

_____

_____

_____

This week I am thankful for

_____

_____

_____

_____

_____

_____

_____

Special thoughts

_____

_____

_____

_____

_____

_____

CHAPTER 6

Rejoice

Though the demands and circumstances of the day are prone to shift without much warning, you have hope as an anchor. Being tied to the steadiness and stability of God allows your joy to be rooted much deeper than the everyday happenings that attempt to sway you or cloud your perspective. In this reciprocal relationship, where you delight in God and God in you, there is never a shortage of things to rejoice over.

My strength
is in the

quietness
and confidence
of God's
presence

God

will fill you with

joy

and

peace

We rejoice
in the
hope
and
glory
of God

And again I say, Rejoice

I shall go out with joy and be led by peace

God
will
rejoice
over you with
singing

Hold fast in hope

175

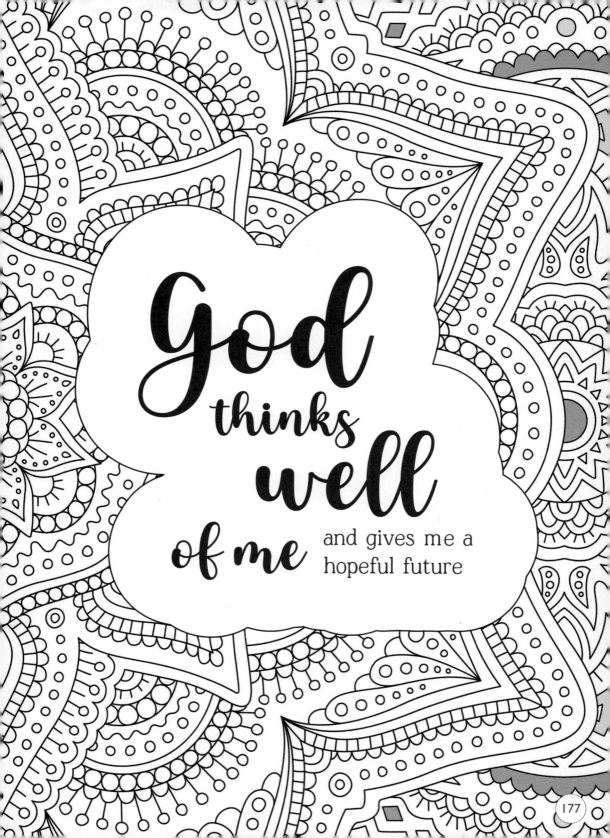

God
thinks
well
of me and gives me a
hopeful future

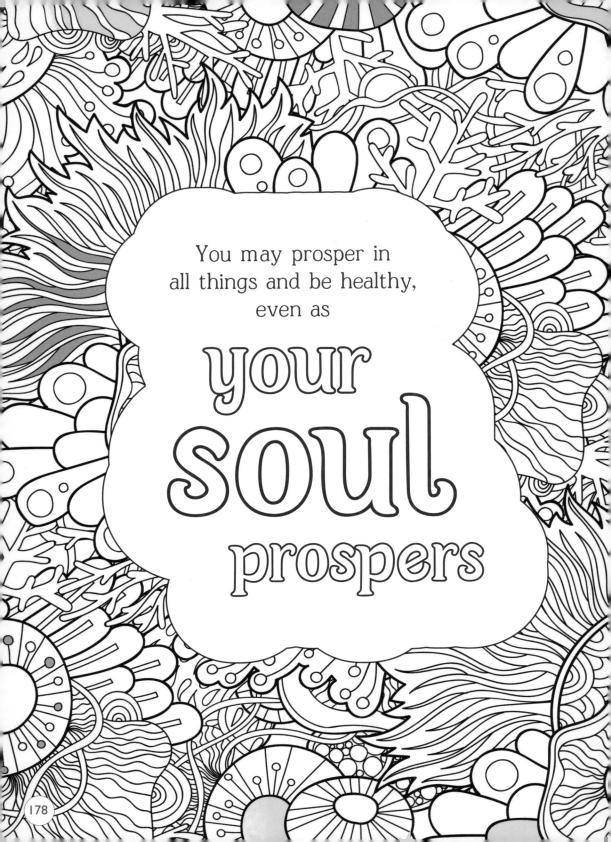

You may prosper in
all things and be healthy,
even as

your
soul
prospers

Always rejoice. Pray without ceasing. *In everything give thanks*

Delight in God,

and he will give you the desires of your heart

Page 163
ISAIAH 30:15 (WEB)

Your strength will be in quietness and in confidence.

How might this type of strength lead to joy?

_____

_____

_____

_____

_____

_____

_____

This week I am thankful for   *Special thoughts*

_____   _____

_____   _____

_____   _____

_____   _____

_____   _____

_____   _____

_____   _____

_____   _____

Page 164
ROMANS 15:13 *(WEB)*

Now may the God of hope fill you with all joy and peace in believing, that you may abound in hope, in the power of the Holy Spirit.

_____

_____

_____

_____

_____

_____

Page 167
ROMANS 5:2–5 *(KJV)*

By [him] we have access by faith into this grace wherein we stand, and rejoice in hope of the glory of God.
And not only so, but we glory in tribulations also: knowing that tribulation worketh patience;
And patience, experience; and experience, hope:
And hope maketh not ashamed; because the love of God is shed abroad in our hearts by the Holy Ghost which is given unto us.

_____

_____

_____

_____

_____

_____

Page 169
PHILIPPIANS 4:4 (KJV)

Rejoice in the Lord always: and again I say, Rejoice.

List three things that you can rejoice about today.

_____
_____
_____
_____
_____
_____
_____
_____

This week I am thankful for

_____
_____
_____
_____
_____
_____
_____

Special thoughts

_____
_____
_____
_____
_____
_____
_____

Page 171

ISAIAH 55:12 *(DRA)*

For you shall go out with joy, and be led forth with peace: the mountains and the hills shall sing praise before you, and all the trees of the country shall clap their hands.

Page 173

ZEPHANIAH 3:17 *(WEB)*

God is among you, a mighty one who will save. He will rejoice over you with joy. He will calm you in his love. He will rejoice over you with singing.

Page 174
HEBREWS 10:22–23 *(WEB)*

Let's draw near with a true heart in fullness of faith, having our hearts sprinkled from an evil conscience, and having our body washed with pure water, let's hold fast the confession of our hope without wavering; for he who promised is faithful.

_____

_____

_____

_____

_____

_____

Page 177
JEREMIAH 29:11 *(WEB)*

"For I know the thoughts that I think toward you," says God, "thoughts of peace, and not of evil, to give you hope and a future."

_____

_____

_____

_____

_____

_____

Page 178
3 JOHN 1:2 (WEB)

Beloved, I pray that you may prosper in all things and be healthy, even as your soul prospers.

List three things you can do to help your soul prosper.

_____

_____

_____

_____

_____

_____

This week I am thankful for

_____

_____

_____

_____

_____

_____

_____

Special thoughts

_____

_____

_____

_____

_____

_____

Page 181

1 THESSALONIANS 5:16–18 *(WEB)*

Always rejoice. Pray without ceasing. In everything give thanks, for this is the will of God in Christ Jesus toward you.

When in life is this easy and when is it hard? List the ways, pray, and give thanks in all!

_____

_____

_____

_____

_____

_____

This week I am thankful for

_____

_____

_____

_____

_____

_____

_____

Special thoughts

_____

_____

_____

_____

_____

_____

_____

Page 183

PSALM 37:3–4 (WEB)

Trust in God, and do good.
    Dwell in the land, and enjoy safe pasture.
Also delight yourself in God,
    and he will give you the desires of your heart.

List three ways you can take more delight in God.

_____

_____

_____

_____

_____

This week I am thankful for

_____

_____

_____

_____

_____

_____

Special thoughts

_____

_____

_____

_____

_____

_____

CHAPTER 7

Live in the Present

You received the gift of salvation and abundant, eternal life the moment you first believed. There now lies within you an ability to simultaneously hold eternal perspective and see the intricate beauty and power held in the present moment. When regrets over the past or anxieties over the future threaten your peace, let your soul rest in these verses, which remind you of the unchangeable truth of God living in you and the spiritual provision that it brings.

Don't be
anxious
for
tomorrow

My soul is anchored and steadfast

I am
transformed
and
renewed

Walking *in* wisdom, I redeem my time

I have learned in whatever state I am, to be content

203

Think
on the
good
things

Behold, all things have become new

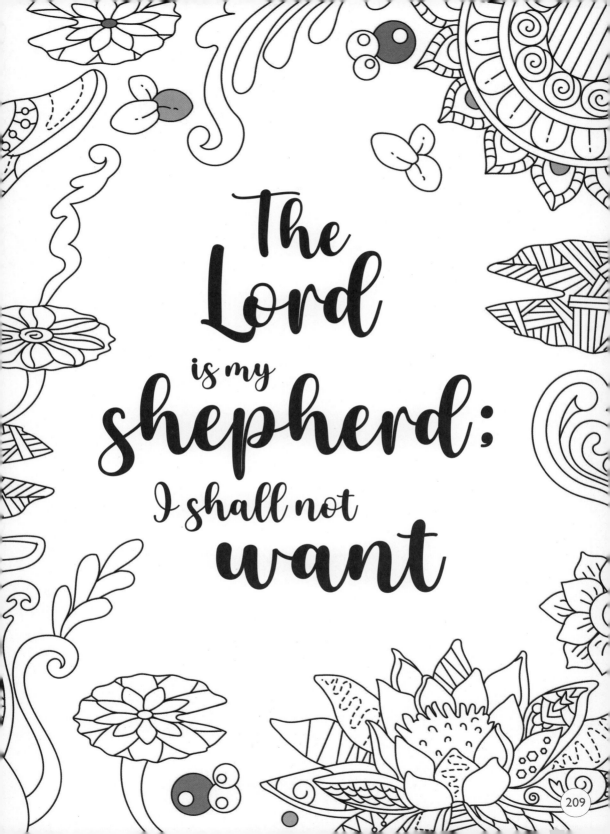

The Lord is my shepherd: I shall not want

Give
us
this day our
daily
bread

Goodness and loving kindness

shall follow me all
the days of my life

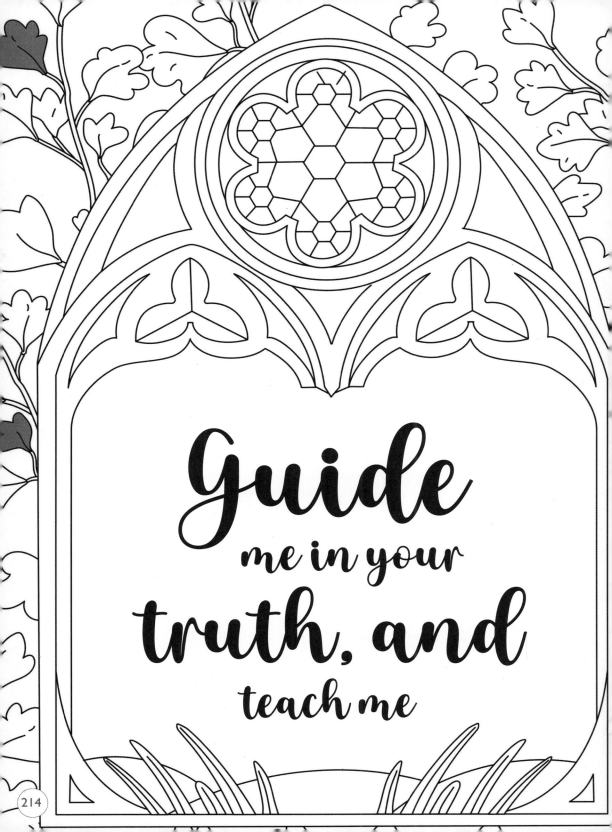

Guide me in your truth, and teach me

MATTHEW 6:34 (WEB)

But seek first God's Kingdom and his righteousness; and all these things will be given to you as well.

How does accepting that each day has its own difficulties free you to be present?

_____

_____

_____

_____

_____

_____

This week I am thankful for

_____

_____

_____

_____

_____

_____

_____

_____

Special thoughts

_____

_____

_____

_____

_____

_____

_____

_____

Page 197
HEBREWS 6:18–19 (YLT)

Through two immutable things, in which [it is] impossible
for God to lie, a strong comfort we may have who did
flee for refuge to lay hold on the hope set before [us],
which we have, as an anchor of the soul, both sure and steadfast.

_____

_____

_____

_____

_____

Page 198
ROMANS 12:2 (WEB)

Don't be conformed to this world, but be transformed by the renewing of
your mind, so that you may prove what is the good, well-pleasing, and perfect
will of God.

_____

_____

_____

_____

_____

_____

Page 201
EPHESIANS 5:15–16 *(WEB)*

Therefore watch carefully how you walk, not as unwise, but as wise, redeeming the time.

List three areas in which you can live more mindfully, and pray for wisdom in doing so.

_____

_____

_____

_____

_____

_____

This week I am thankful for   *Special thoughts*

_____   _____

_____   _____

_____   _____

_____   _____

_____   _____

_____   _____

_____   _____

_____   _____

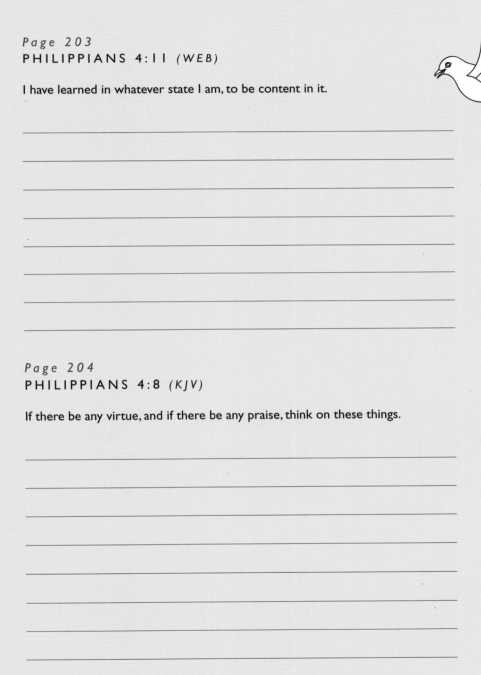

PHILIPPIANS 4:11 *(WEB)*

I have learned in whatever state I am, to be content in it.

_____

_____

_____

_____

_____

_____

_____

_____

PHILIPPIANS 4:8 *(KJV)*

If there be any virtue, and if there be any praise, think on these things.

_____

_____

_____

_____

_____

_____

_____

_____

2 CORINTHIANS 5:17 *(WEB)*

Therefore if anyone is in Christ, he is a new creation. The old things have passed away. Behold, all things have become new.

Give thanks for a few ways in which you are a new creation and unlike your former self.

_____

_____

_____

_____

_____

_____

This week I am thankful for   *Special thoughts*

Page 209
PSALM 23:1–3 (WEB)

God is my shepherd:
  I shall lack nothing.
He makes me lie down in green pastures.
  He leads me beside still waters.
He restores my soul.

How does trusting God's provision free you to live in the present?

_____

_____

_____

_____

_____

This week I am thankful for

_____

_____

_____

_____

_____

_____

_____

Special thoughts

_____

_____

_____

_____

_____

_____

_____

Page 210
MATTHEW 6:9–13 (WEB)

Our Father in heaven, may your name be kept holy.
Let your Kingdom come.
Let your will be done on earth as it is in heaven.
Give us today our daily bread.
Forgive us our debts,
as we also forgive our debtors.
Bring us not into temptation,
but deliver us from the evil one.
For yours is the Kingdom, the power, and the glory forever. Amen.

_____

_____

_____

_____

_____

Page 213
PSALM 23:6 (WEB)

Surely goodness and loving kindness shall follow
   me all the days of my life,
and I will dwell in God's house forever.

_____

_____

_____

_____

_____

Page 214
PSALM 25:4–5 *(WEB)*

Show me your ways, God.
  Teach me your paths.
Guide me in your truth, and teach me,
  For you are the God of my salvation,
  I wait for you all day long.

How does learning from God lessen your worry and fear over the past and future?

_____

_____

_____

_____

_____

This week I am thankful for   *Special thoughts*

_____   _____

_____   _____

_____   _____

_____   _____

_____   _____

_____   _____

_____   _____

About the Author

Rachel Mayew is the writer and Christian meditation teacher behind Holistic Faith Lifestyle, a website and blog dedicated to helping others experience God within the five aspects of holistic health: mind, body, spirit, emotions, and relationships. She creates every blog post, YouTube meditation, affirmation, and scriptural resource to help you seek the sacred in the everyday.

Credits

Bible Verses

The verses used within this book have been taken from the *Darby Bible (DBY)*, *Douay–Rheims 1899 American Edition (DRA)*, *Douay–Rheims Bible (DRB)*, the *King James Version (KJV)*, the *World English Bible (WEB)*, and *Young's Literal Translation (YLT)*, all of which are in the public domain.

Images